BEING HEAR

A BOOK ABOUT BEING PRESENT AND LISTENING

EARS FOR EYES

Scott Boms · An Introduction

In my early teens, I was introduced to a comic book artist named Ty Templeton through a mutual friend. Although we fell out of touch in subsequent years, Ty imparted a valuable piece of advice to me that I still think about often—*to be present and pay attention*. To listen with your eyes and ears. To consider how these senses can paint a richer story, enable more nuanced observation, and clearer understanding of needs, desires, and motivations.

While presence and observation are part of the underlying connective tissue, the heart of this book is about listening. Its origin is owed to Ethan Stock, who at Q&A, following the U.S. election, asked a simple yet poignant question, *"How can we give people ears?"*

Ethan's question stuck with me and brought back Ty's advice. It took some time to understand just how meaningful a question it truly was and what we could do with it—an important point in itself.

Our modern world has largely been reshaped around immediacy, instant gratification, and platforms where everyone is in competition to be acknowledged and heard. A place where it's increasingly difficult to find a signal in the sea of noise, and where the inherent social responsibility of these new communication tools and platforms looms large.

How could products we create encourage people to become better, more sincere listeners? How do our environment and expectations of each other affect how we behave?

Consider for a moment how the pace of progress today has made it so easy to unintentionally interrupt a colleague because we're constantly watching the clock or have to rush off to another meeting. Or how these new digital experiences often unintentionally encourage a lack of genuine presence yet demand an immediacy in responsiveness—a like, a comment or a counter-argument, rather than the necessary space to experience moments through all our senses and be thoughtful if and when a response is warranted. How can we instead enjoy the moment, and be more aware when and how our biases influence our behaviors? We rarely give ourselves permission to not have something to say. To listen—not to respond—but to just *listen*.

Our hope is that the themes woven throughout this book, and expressed through Fuchsia MacAree's delightfully curious illustrations, will take you on a journey and encourage you to ask questions—of others and yourself—about listening, about how to be more present and generous in life, and ultimately give you new patterns, tools and techniques to make connections that can bring us all closer to a shared understanding of ourselves and the world.

WE HAVE
TWO EARS AND
ONE MOUTH
SO THAT WE
CAN LISTEN
TWICE AS MUCH
AS WE SPEAK

EPICTETUS, C. 50AD – 135AD

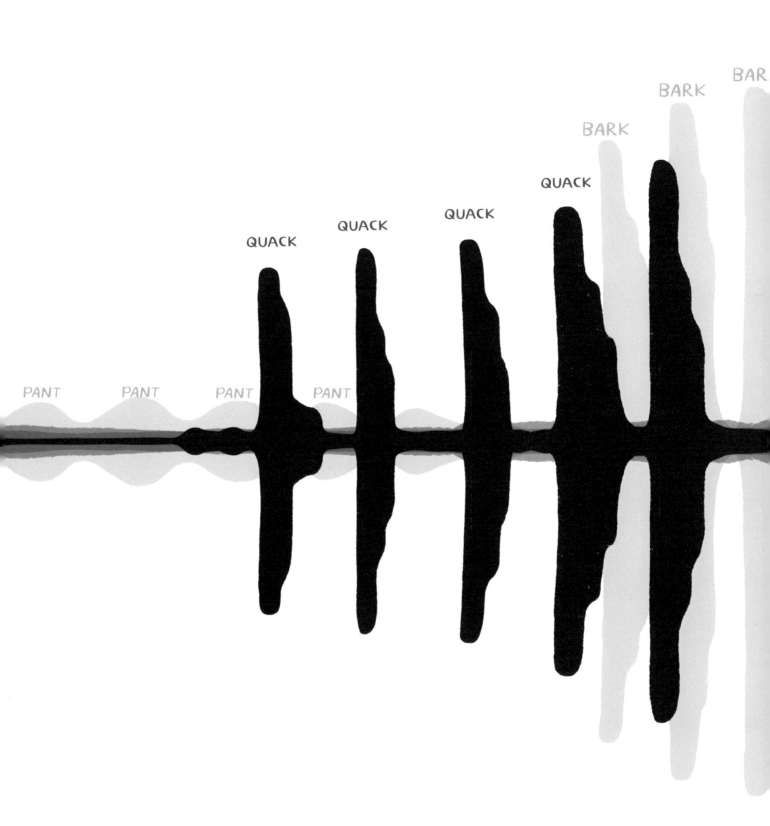

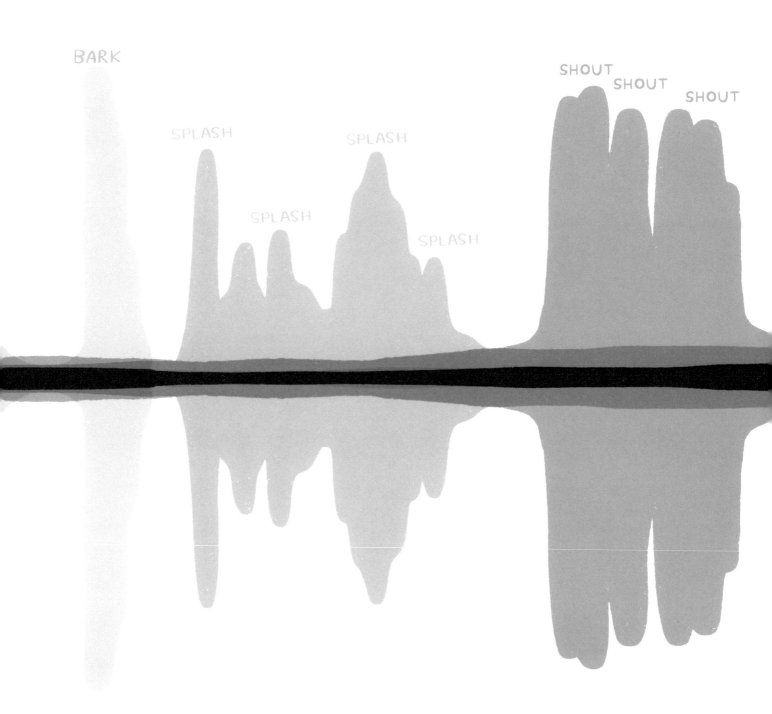

EVERYBODY SHOULD BE QUIET NEAR A LITTLE STREAM AND LISTEN

SILENT

SILETN

SLIETN

LSIETN

LSITEN

LISTEN

COMMUNICATION IS THE JOB

Boz · December 29, 2016

There are a lot of people who build things in Silicon Valley. They spend their time writing code or designing flows or building models. But how do they know what to build? Well, they work with a group of people whose job is to connect them with the information they need to answer that question. Those connectors in turn work with people whose job is to collect that information in the first place. This pattern repeats throughout.

The success of all these information connectors and collectors depends on precisely one skill: *communication*.

Each of us are always communicating. Try as we might, we cannot help it. Saying nothing can often be even more damaging than saying the wrong thing. The people around us are so eager to understand the world around them that in the absence of true communication, they will attempt to find a signal in noise. None of us gets to control what others are hearing or how they are interpreting things. We can only control what we contribute to that milieu.

Given that we cannot prevent communication, we must embrace it. While perfect communication is impossible, my goal is to get most people most of the information most of the time. Here are some strategies I employ.

Layer Your Message

If you take away one thing from this post I hope it is that communication is important and unavoidable. Beyond that I have a numbered list of eight tips with short descriptions. Beyond those I have longer explanations of each. The structure of this post is not an accident, it is a model for getting your message across to a large audience whose level of engagement in the content will vary. The same is true of meetings or all-hands where we tend to have one topic or theme and then several points we plan to cover, and then we lay out the detailed content. The larger the audience, the more this type of structure becomes important as the variance in interest levels only grows. People have to be able to engage at their level of interest and get value—and progressively learn whether or not they want to invest more—so it can't be all or nothing.

Consider the Second Order Audience

You aren't just communicating to those who attend your meeting or read your posts and emails. You are also communicating to the set of people that everyone in your audience talks to subsequently. Focusing your message into a format that is readily repeatable by others with high fidelity can be a huge advantage, especially if you can distill it down to short memorable phrases.

Communicate Defensively

You need to consider the most cynical interpretation of your message before you say anything. For audiences of any reasonable size there will be someone inclined to take the most critical possible interpretation of your words. If you give them enough space, that person will build a logical (but incorrect) interpretation. If they then share it with others that becomes a de facto communication that you are responsible for even if you never said, or intended, it. So before you communicate take the time to consider all parts of your audience and how you might be misinterpreted and then refine your message to reduce the likelihood of miscommunication.

Repetition is Key

Advertisers have known for a long time that ensuring someone hears a critical message several times is key to them retaining it. Within any given communication be sure to keep tying things back to the critical message. In the case of this post, the idea that communication is unavoidable is something I mention several times. Including just there.

Use Multiple Channels

People absorb information differently through different

media so if you want to ensure you've really reached everyone it is wise to get your message out on many different ways. In this case I gave a talk on this in person to some colleagues and am now writing a post. With some individuals I'll probably also raise this one on one. For important All Hands meetings we will even create posters in the Facebook Analog Laboratory that mirror the themes to even take advantage of physical space around us to communicate. This also helps with the goal of repetition.

Maintain Channels

All the right text is worthless if nobody reads it. Building and maintaining strong channels of communication is critical to being able to communicate effectively. If you wait until you need such channels, you are already too late. All Hands and meetings are somewhat easier because you can control an invite list and, to some extent, influence people's calendars. For written communication we invest a lot in maintaining Facebook Groups but other companies might us email lists or channels. The important thing with broadcast channels is that people know if something important happens, they will read about it there. It is equally important that the communication there be exclusively content we think is important to almost all of the audience or people will tune it out. The channels also have to be used frequently enough to stay well ranked in peoples inboxes and feeds, so investing in regular, high-quality content production is important.

Communicate Early and Often

The most common mistake I see is leaders waiting to say anything until they are certain what they are communicating is absolutely correct. That sounds laudable but in practice it tends to slows down communication dramatically and gives space for the rumor mill to run amok. In my experience, people would rather hear about the current state of our understanding and have it revised as we learn more than hear nothing at all. People can deal with imperfect information but they cannot stand information insecurity.

Debug Miscommunication

When I'm doing a poor job of communicating it can feel like I'm pushing with a rope. I have some clear vision in my head and people just aren't doing what I expect. It can be a frustrating experience and it is tempting to blame the audience for not understanding. But make no mistake, when this happens, it is your fault. You have to sit down and ask questions from a place of humility to hear what they took away from what you said. Take full responsibility for any discrepancy from what you intended and make corrections with your entire audience.

I think that a lot of the reason people fail to communicate well is that they aren't comfortable with their responsibility. Whether they be leaders or managers, many would much rather imagine themselves as just a part of the team. Unfortunately, that isn't an option and indulging the fantasy is irresponsible because you let people down who are counting on you to step up. Even if you don't think you're a leader or a manager, you're still a communicator. We are all leaders to someone whether we like it or not. People are looking to us. We don't have the capacity not to communicate. So let's invest to do it well.

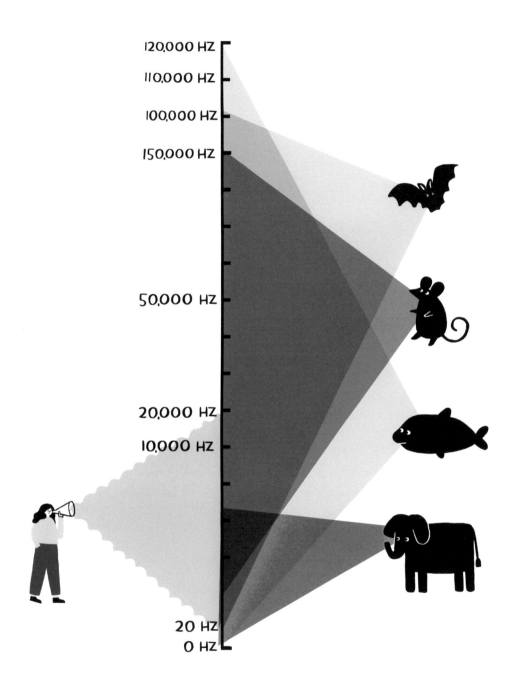

120,000 HZ
110,000 HZ
100,000 HZ
150,000 HZ
50,000 HZ
20,000 HZ
10,000 HZ
20 HZ
0 HZ

WHAT WE CAN'T HEAR

Did you forget to
put on makeup today? You
look spectacular

She is Beyonce's
sister. What did the user
see? We're in Man Bun.

I need some coffee
Is there no Queen in Ireland?
There is risotto!

HAIKUS MADE FROM
SNIPPETS OF OVERHEARD
CONVERSATION IN MPK,
NEW YORK AND DUBLIN

I didn't come here
to be alone. Is that a
nipple or hickey?

I met her friend who
was super cute and who I
was trying to date

Celebrate good times
Come on! Hangovers get worse
as you get older

Oh shit! So from now
on only noughties kids will
be graduating?

INFORMATION DIVERSITY & UNFOLLOWING

Lada Adamic · August 15, 2016

"The top post overall resulting in liberals unfollowing other liberals and the top political post causing conservatives to unfollow other conservatives was (ironically) a video asking people to listen to the other side because they might learn something."

Anecdotally, people report unfollowing Facebook friends because of their political posting. Here's what the data says:

-→ While cross-affiliation (liberal/conservative) friendships constitute 20-25% of friendships, they represent 41.5% of user-to-user unfollowing in feed.

-→ The top 5+ posts resulting in liberal to conservative or conservative to liberal unfollowing are political.

-→ The top post overall resulting in liberals unfollowing other liberals and the top political post causing conservatives to unfollow other conservatives was (ironically) a video asking people to listen to the other side because they might learn something.

This is the result of two convenience samples: feed unfollows July 4–31st, together with the original content IDs for reshares, and a set of people who are likely liberal or conservative based on the self identified political views they enter into their profile or if they follow a popular liberal or conservative Facebook page (ad-hoc data methodology described here).

During this ~4 week period, 7.3% of liberals and 10.3% of conservatives had unfollowed at least one other person. Since the original sample of politically affiliated people had more liberals, this still left 4.4M liberals and 3.1M conservatives who had unfollowed at least one person. Liberals unfollowed 16.9M others, conservatives 14.1M.

It is striking that the top posts in raw volume leading people to unfollow cross-ideology friends are political (even though in principle they could be on any topic…). There is likely additional impact in unfriending (since the volume of unfriending to unfollowing is 10:1). However, this was only a look at people's unwillingness to listen to the other side, and the overall volume of unfollowing is relatively low (it's hard to know what a healthy amount of unfollowing might be). Finally, there is a lot of benefit in cross-ideological discussion prompted by posts (though maybe not the more confrontational of these…), and ongoing research into how pages and groups complement timeline posts in supporting (civil) political discourse.

13M (or 42.8%) of this combined set of unfollowed accounts were in the sample of politically affiliated people.

I AM LISTENING

Ramya Sethuraman · October 29, 2015

"I have a pretty long question, so I don't mind waiting till the end", the lady with glasses said, handing off the microphone to the next person in line. I had just wrapped up my talk on Empathy and Accessibility at the Grace Hopper Conference and was answering questions that followed from the audience. This particular lady waited for her turn patiently and then launched into her rather long story.

She had been tagging her personal photos on Facebook in a rush and had ended up tagging people she did not mean to tag inadvertently. She described how she had tried to untag people and thought she had untagged them from the photos but that was not the case. She was visibly upset and asked, "I can imagine how this might be even more complicated for people that are blind. You talk about empathy and caring about accessibility, how do you account for issues like this?"

I paused and thanked her for bringing up this issue, apologized for what she had to go through and methodically tried to address the issue. I offered our help center channels where she can describe the specifics of what happened and get help, I offered to talk to her offline to get all the details to create a task, I addressed her specific accessibility question explaining how it will actually be harder for someone using a screen reader to tag a person by mistake using the keyboard.

None of this resonated with her though. She continued to hold the microphone and add additional minor details of how she had tagged people by mistake and how frustrating it was. She then asked, "Imagine if my grandmother tagged someone by mistake, wouldn't that be even harder for her?"

Finally, I said, "I understand how frustrating this must have been for you. I know I would be really annoyed if I tagged a bunch of people I did not want to tag on my photos. I am sorry you had to go through this experience. Yes, it will be even harder for your grandmother if she landed in this situation. For our part, we will consider including more people in different age categories in our usability testing if we don't already do that. Thank you for bringing this up."

And then she nodded, smiled and handed the microphone to the next person.

She wanted to be heard and wanted someone to acknowledge how difficult her experience had been, how she had felt then. She wanted to know that I was really listening to her story.

I finally was.

I had missed a crucial step in our interaction. The listening and acknowledging. I had moved on to problem solving and next steps.

And when I really listened and told her I understood, she was happy.

I was finally listening.

INTERRUPTING

Debbie Ferguson · Wednesday May 17, 2017

"I'm feeling really really low right now. I'm now meant to be working on another product where the 4 others are men. Every meeting I've been in this week I've been cut off, I've not been allowed to speak. I just came out of a meeting where I was the only women out of more than 12 people.

Again I wasn't allowed to speak, I was cut off to the point where I had to ask if we were on mute. Then I heard another person say the exact thing I said and be heard and also be given credit. I just cried in the bathroom for like 10 min. I just feel so incredibly helpless."

—*from a co-worker*

This is not a new topic. But, unfortunately, I hear versions of this story far too often and regularly. When I was a man, I wish I had been more sensitive to the issue. As a woman, I've experienced it (although probably to a lesser degree than others) and it is incredibly demotivating. Why try if I'm not going to be heard? Why suggest an idea if it won't be seriously considered until repeated by someone else in the room?

Adam Grant talks about the value of both having non-conformists AND encouraging them to contribute as the key to building a culture of originality. Shutting people down kills this. If you are on a team where this is happening, the team is being impaired and handicapped. It is missing out on a wider set of perspectives which inevitably leads to decisions that are not as good as they could have been. Over time, your team will lose those voices permanently. Which will permanently limit your potential. Quite simply, there's no point in having a diversity of experiences on your team if they are not listened to.

If you are an interrupter, there is great news. You can fix it! Stop! Listen. That's all you have to do.

If you aren't, first make sure you aren't. You may be surprised to discover you are. Secondly, you can make sure others don't interrupt. Stop them! Pay attention to when someone seems to be interested in speaking and create space for them to speak up. Its a skill, but not a hard one to do. Pay attention to what's happening with body language and extra close attention to those on VC.

Be the ally. It's in everyone's best interest. Even the interrupter's.

IF  YOU ARE

AN INTERRUPTER,

THERE IS GREAT NEWS.

YOU CAN FIX IT!

STOP! LISTEN.

THAT'S ALL YOU

HAVE TO DO.

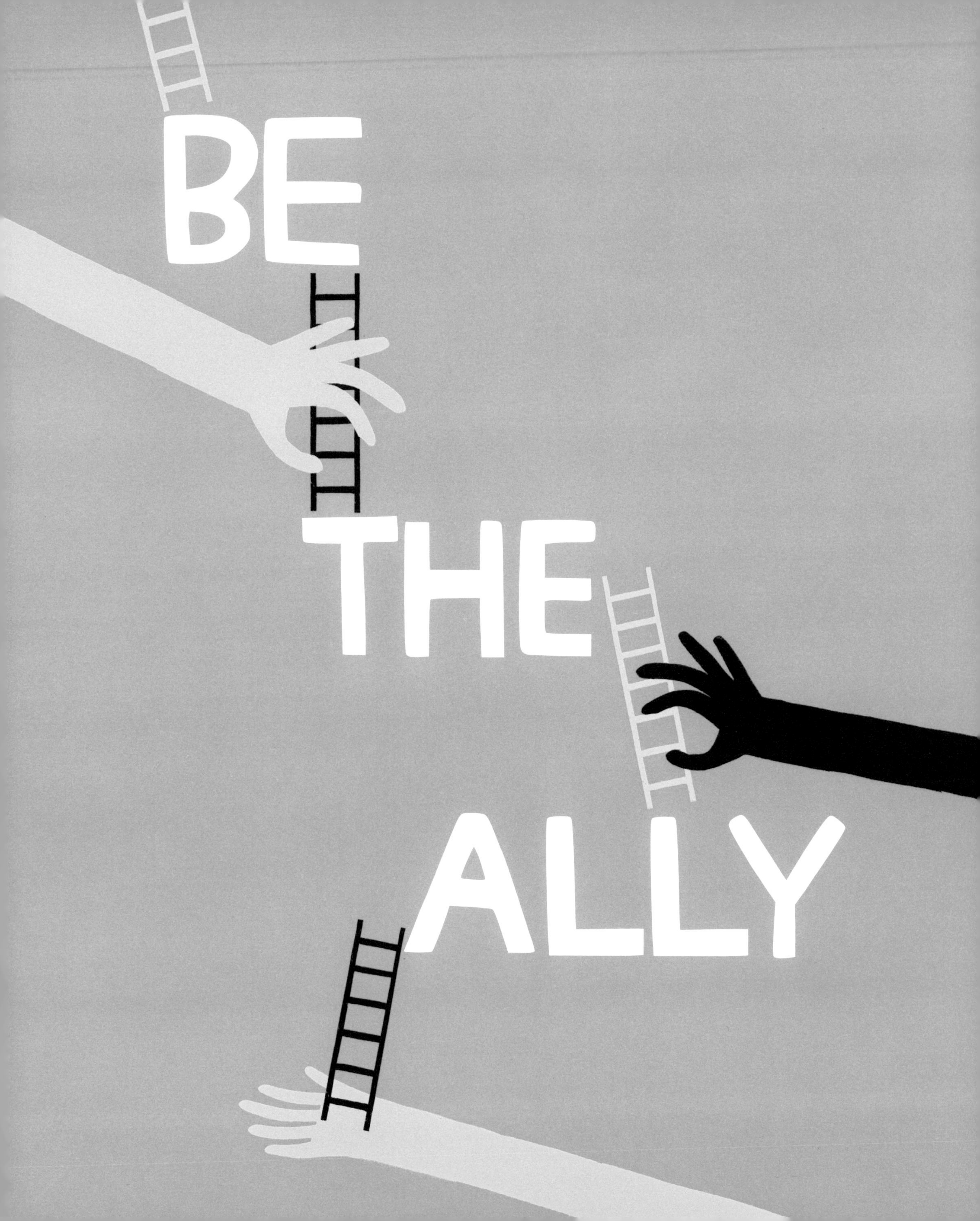
BE
THE
ALLY

POINT IT OUT

Notice it

What is the tone of communication used?
What body language are people displaying?
(eye contact, posture, etc.)

Name it

"I noticed that…"
"It seems like…"

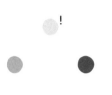

CHECK IT OUT

Clarify it

"Did I read that right?"
"Is there something I'm missing?"

Validate It

"I know I can't understand what you experienced, but that must have been so hard for you to sit through."

WORK IT OUT

State an intention of support

"I'm here to support you in any way that I can be effective in."

Problem solve together

"What could be a first step to clear the difficulty about this situation?"

SEASHELL RESONANCE

There is a popular folk myth that if one holds a seashell—specifically a conch shell—to one's ear, one can hear the sound of the ocean.

The rushing sound that one hears is in fact the noise of the surrounding environment, resonating within the cavity of the shell. The same effect can be produced with any resonant cavity, such as an empty cup or even by simply cupping one's hand over one's ear. The similarity of the noise produced by the resonator to that of the oceans is due to the resemblance between ocean movements and airflow.

The resonator is simply attenuating some frequencies of the ambient noise in the environment, including air flowing within the resonator and sound originating within the human body itself more than other sounds.

The human ear picks up sounds made by the human body as well, including the sounds of blood flowing and muscles acting. These sounds are normally discarded by the brain; however, they become more obvious when louder external sounds are filtered out. This occlusion effect occurs with seashells, cups, or hands held over one's ears, and also with circumaural headphones, whose cups form a seal around the ear, raising the acoustic impedance to external sounds.

FLUTE LYREBIRDS

The Australian superb lyrebird (*Menura novaehollandiae*) is an expert in mimicry and during the summer breeding season, may sing for hours a day. Lyrebirds can imitate natural and artificial sounds from their environment, including chainsaws, camera shutters, phone ringtones, and even perfectly rendering those of other bird species, weaving them into complex songs.

In the early 1900s, a lyrebird chick raised in captivity who had overheard songs played by its owner on a flute, over time incorporated parts of those tunes into its repertoire. Because lyrebirds are capable of carrying two tunes at once, and only years later after being released into the nearby National Park, it was discovered that this lyrebird had passed those songs down to a generation of other birds, earning the name "flute lyrebirds."

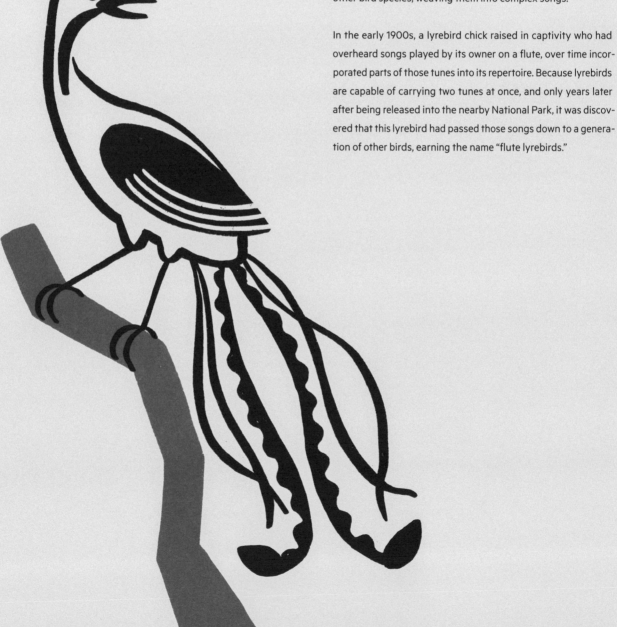

SONG OF THE HUMPBACK WHALE

Baleen whales, which include the humpback and blue whale species, are known for their almost musical songs which can travel for great distances. These sequences of predictable, repeating moans and whistles are thought to communicate health and youthfulness during mating season and human-like emotional nuance when observed during times of loss or mourning within a pod.

The eerie melodic qualities of sounds produced by humpback whales can reach 188 decibels and the low frequency vibrations from them can be felt many miles away. These sounds, louder than the sound produced by the average jet aircraft, are considered to be the most complex non-human form of communication known.

In 2006, researchers unexpectedly discovered that populations of whales observed on both sides of the Southern Indian ocean sang different tunes.

Answer key can be found
inside the back cover

Thomas Edison plays "Mary's Little Lamb" on a strip of tinfoil wrapped around a spinning cylinder.

1877

Guglielmo Marconi sends the first transatlantic signal—the Morse code signal for the letter "S".

1901

Commercial FM radio broadcasting begins in the U.S.

1941

1875

Alexander Graham Bell makes the first sound transmission

1887

Emile Berliner patents the flat-disc gramophone, making the production of multiple copies practical.

1927

The Jazz Singer is released as the first commercial talking picture.

Robert Moog shows elements of his early music synthesizers.

1965

Sony introduces the Walk-man, a palm-sized stereo cassette tape player.

1980

The first MP3 players for downloadable internet audio appear.

1997

1948

The microgroove 33–⅓ RPM long-play vinyl record (LP) is introduced by Columbia Records.

1977

NASA launch the Voyager spacecraft carrying the Golden Record time capsule.

1982

Sony releases the first compact disc (CD) player.

AN (INCOMPLETE) TIMELINE OF SOUND

THE OLDEST RECORDED PERSON WAS BORN THE YEAR ALEXANDER GRAHAM BELL
MADE THE 1ST SOUND TRANSMISSION & DIED THE YEAR THE MP3 PLAYER WAS RELEASED

UNTRANSLATABLE WORDS

tartle, *n, Scottish*
The act of hesitating while introducing someone because you've forgotten their name.

ghiqq, *n, Persian*
The sound made by a boiling kettle.

gokotta, *n, Swedish*
Literally "dawn picnic"
To wake up early to hear the birdsong.

psithurism, *n, English*
(archaic) The sound of leaves rustling in the trees.

yaourter, *v, French*
Literally "to yogurt"
Attempting to speak or sing in a foreign language that one doesn't know very well; it often involves throwing in nonsense sounds or words when one needs to fill in the blanks.

fýrgebræc, *n, Old English*
The crackling sound made by a fire.

prozvonit, *v, Czech*
To initiate a phone call and stop it before the call is picked, to inform the receiver of something without having to pay for the call.

μυγμός, *n, Ancient Greek*
A moaning or whimpering noise, particularly one made when someone is trying to wake you up.

When people talk, listen completely. Don't be thinking what you're going to say. <u>Most people never listen. Nor do they observe.</u> You should be able to go into a room, and when you come out, know everything that you saw there and not only that. If that room gave you any feeling you should know exactly what it was that gave you that feeling.

ERNEST HEMINGWAY'S ADVICE ON WRITING

REMOVING PEOPLE WHO HAVE DIED FROM INSENSITIVE PRODUCT EXPERIENCES

Moira Burke · January 11, 2017

Only about 3% of the people with Facebook accounts who have died have had their accounts memorialized. As a result, the names of deceased sometimes appear in PYMK, On this Day, and other product experiences in ways that may upset their friends. To remedy this, we've built a classifier to identify people who have likely died but whose accounts haven't been memorialized with greater than 95% accuracy. In the future we can use this classifier's output to hide these people's names as if they were memorialized, and raise awareness of different options to their friends (including memorialization, account deletion, legacy contacts, and/or leaving the account alone).

This is a joint project within the Safety and Compassion team within Protect and Care (PAC), including: Mark Handel, Jed Brubaker (U. Colorado), Dan Muriello, Vanessa Callison-Burch, and Dave Pawson.

Which Features Matter?

Overall, we try to distinguish memorialized accounts from accounts that are inactive for other reasons, such as abandoned accounts stuck in checkpoints or general churn.

FIRST, THE OBVIOUS FEATURES:

→ Longer times since their last action

→ Logged in fewer days in the past month (lower L28). This can be non-zero if an account has been memorialized for less than 28 days

→ Fewer or no self profile views in the past 28 days, and over the past 18 months

→ More terms like *"miss you"* and *"heaven"* on their wall Mark built a list of terms (the "memtext dictionary")

that best distinguish memorialized and non-memorialized accounts, so the process is language-agnostic and can be internationalized relatively easily.

→ Tagged in fewer/no things in the past 28 days

→ Older people are more likely than younger people

AND SOME SURPRISING FEATURES WE'RE EXPLORING:

Religious posts. The classifier confuses general religious language with terms in our memtext dictionary (e.g, "heaven"). So, we include the ratio of posts by the focal person that include words from the memtext dictionary to posts by others with memtext language (calculated across all posts). The higher this ratio, the more likely it is that the person is religious rather than deceased.

People with a religion listed are less likely to have memorialized accounts. Despite being a proxy for knowing how to use features, it is also consistent with past research that people who belong to organized groups, including religions, live longer. We include a binary variable in the model indicating whether the person listed a religion in their profile (but not which religion).

Fewer wall posts from others (in the past 28 days, and over all time). This is consistent with past research showing that "popular" people live longer. Posts on memorialized accounts tend to cluster around birthdays, holidays, and anniversaries of their death, so wall posts are less likely to occur in the past month, unless there was a recent holiday.

A higher single-day spike in profile views by friends over the past 18 months. Memorialized accounts have

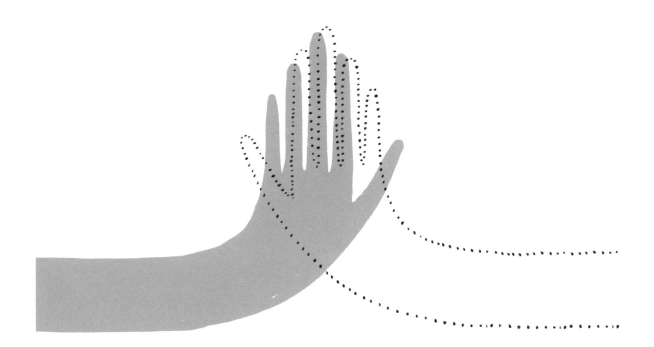

higher spikes in profile views on a single day than non-memorialized accounts; they also cluster on birthdays, holidays, and anniversaries of the death. Surprisingly, non-memorialized accounts don't have a "birthday view spike" any more. People now write "happy birthday" now without visiting the recipient's timeline.

More broadcast posts and self-views on their own wall. It could be that people who look at their own wall a lot have higher levels of self-regulation or anxiety (which can be harmful to health/longevity) or it could be that people who look at their own wall a lot are highly engaged (I'm guessing this is the right interpretation). If it's the latter, their friends are also likely to be engaged and thus know how to trigger memorialization when needed.

SI checkpoints for security, access, and education: Accounts currently stuck in checkpoints are less likely to be memorialized (they're more likely to be living people who tried to get into their own accounts but had trouble). SI checkpoints for fake accounts didn't seem to add value, surprisingly.

Single people, engaged, widowed, and divorced people are more likely to have memorialized accounts than people who haven't specified their relationship status. "Engaged" is the surprise here—married people live longer, so you'd think that engaged people do, too.

ADDITIONAL FIELDS THAT WE SHOULDN'T INCLUDE IN THE CLASSIFIER:

These are all proxies for engagement and likely technical savvy, and are all significantly associated with being memorialized. Since we want to identify people who have died but whose accounts haven't been memorialized, we'd most likely leave these features out:

→ Higher friend count

→ Higher tenure

→ More complete profile (more fields filled in, having a profile picture)

Classifier performance

Using a training set of 92,000 accounts in the U.S. (80/20 train/test), roughly half of which were memorialized, we built a classifier that is more than 95% accurate (Precision: 98.2%, Recall: 92.4%). Its accuracy is challenging to measure because this is an example of a "Positive-Unlabeled" (PU) learning problem: We have labeled data for positive cases (memorialized accounts), but unlabeled accounts include people who've died, too (the very people we're trying to find).

MANUAL INSPECTION OF THE FALSE POSITIVES (0.96% OF RESULTS) SUGGEST THAT:

About 35% of them are people who have died but don't have memorialized accounts.

About 25% are completely inactive but have no indications that the person has died (some were caught in checkpoints so owners may have created new accounts).

About 40% are inactive but probably living: friends have tagged them in the past few months while watching sports games/holidays, or have written other things on their walls that don't seem like the person has died.

Next steps

1. We're working with Community Operations to label the borderline unlabeled accounts from our training data to improve classifier performance and reduce false positives.

2. Converting our existing adhoc data analysis into dataswarm pipelines that can run periodically.

3. One feature is expensive: Historic wall post text. There's not a snapshot table in hive, and scraping text in production is expensive. Thankfully, the classifier works well with small slurps of wall posts (e.g., the last 10 posts), so we're looking for opportunities to pull it on demand, such as when a friend writes on the wall. Otherwise we may set up a pipeline to pull historic wall post text at a trickle.

4. We hope to use this classifier to mark accounts as "inferred memorialized" and remove these people's names from the same product experiences where we remove people who have died (such as ads and PYMK).

5. We also hope to learn signals to identify cases where people have died much sooner: within days of the death, so that we can provide appropriate support to their friends and family, making their options clear (including leaving the account alone, memorialization, deleting it, and legacy contacts).

SOMETIMES IT'S A FORM OF LOVE JUST TO TALK TO SOMEBODY THAT YOU HAVE
NOTHING IN COMMON WITH AND STILL BE FASCINATED BY THEIR PRESENCE
—David Byrne

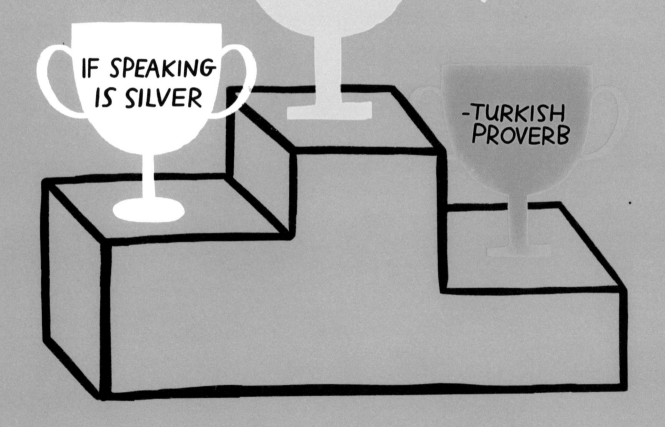

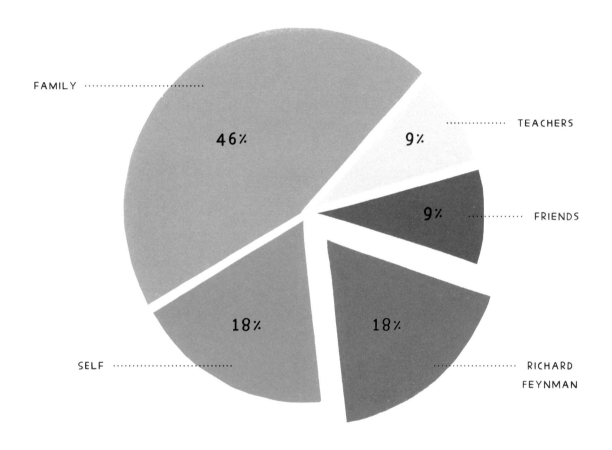

FAMILY
46%

TEACHERS
9%

FRIENDS
9%

SELF
18%

RICHARD
FEYNMAN
18%

SURVEY RESULTS: WHO DO YOU WISH YOU HAD LISTENED TO?

HOW TO BE A GOOD LISTENER

Alain de Botton/The School of Life

Being a good listener is one of the most important and enchanting life-skills anyone can have. Yet, few of us know how to do it, not because we are evil, but because no one has taught us how and—a related point—few have listened sufficiently well to us. So we come to social life greedy to speak rather than listen, hungry to meet others, but reluc-

tant to hear them. Friendship degenerates into a socialized egoism. Like most things, the answer lies in education. Our civilization is full of great books on how to speak—Cicero's Orator and Aristotle's Rhetoric were two of the greatest in the ancient world—but sadly no one has ever written a book called 'The Listener'. There are a range of things that the good listener is doing that makes it so nice to spend time in their company.

Without necessarily quite realizing it, we're often propelled into conversation by something that feels both urgent and somehow undefined. We're bothered at work, we're toying with more ambitious career moves, we're not sure if so and so is right for us; a relationship is in difficulties; we're fretting about something or feeling a bit low about life in general (without being able to put a finger on exactly what's wrong); or perhaps we're very excited and enthusiastic about something—though the reasons for our passion are tricky to pin down. At heart, all these are issues in search of elucidation. The good listener knows that we'd ideally move—via conversation with another person—from a confused agitated state of mind to one that was more focused and (hopefully) more serene. Together with them we'd work out what us really at stake. But, in reality,

this tends not to happen because there isn't enough of an awareness of the desire and need for clarification within conversation. There aren't enough good listeners. So people tend to assert rather than analyze. They restate in many different ways the fact that they are worried, excited, sad or hopeful, and their interlocutor listens but doesn't assist them to discover more.

Good listeners fight against this with a range of conversational gambits. They hover as the other speaks: they offer encouraging little remarks of support, they make gentle positive gestures: a sigh of sympathy, a nod of encouragement, a strategic 'hmm' of interest. All the time they are egging the other to go deeper into issues. They love saying: 'tell me more about …'; 'I was fascinated when you said ..'; 'why did that happen, do you think?' or 'how did you feel about that?' The good listener takes it for granted that they will encounter vagueness in the conversation of others. But they don't condemn, rush or get impatient, because they see vagueness as a universal and highly significant trouble of the mind that it is the task of a true friend to help with. The good listener never forgets how hard—and

how important—it is to know our own minds. Often, we're in the vicinity of something, but we can't quite close in on what's really bothering or exciting us. The good listener knows we hugely benefit from encouragement to elaborate, to go into greater detail, to push a little further. We need someone who, rather than launch forth, will simply say two magic rare words: *Go on...*

You mention a sibling and they want to know a bit

more. What was the relationship like in childhood, how has it changed over time. They're curious where our concerns and excitements come from. They ask thing like: why did that particularly bother you? Why was that such a big thing for you? They keep our histories in mind, they might refer back to something we said before and we feel they're building up a deeper base of engagement. It's fatally easy to say vague things: we simply mention that something is lovely or terrible, nice or annoying. But we don't really explore why we feel this way. The good listener has a productive, friendly suspicion of some of our own first statements and is after the deeper attitudes that are lurking in the background. They take things we say like 'I'm fed up with my job' or 'My partner and I are having a lot of rows...' and help us to concentrate on what it really is about the job we don't like or what the rows might deep down be about.

They're bringing to listening an ambition to clear up underlying issues. They don't just see conversation as the swapping of anecdotes. They are reconnecting the chat

you're having over pizza with the philosophical ambitions of Socrates, whose dialogues are records of his attempts to help his fellow Athenians understand and examine their own underlying ideas and values. A key move of the good listener is not always to follow every byway or sub-plot that the speaker introduces, for they may be getting lost and further from their own point than they would themselves wish. The good listener is helpfully suspicious, knowing

that their purpose is to focus the fundamental themes of the speaker, rather than veering off with them into every side road. They are always looking to take the speaker back to their last reasonable point—saying, 'Yes, yes, but you were saying just a moment ago...'. Or, 'So ultimately, what do you think it was about...' The good listener (paradoxically) is a skilled interrupter. But they don't (as most people do) interrupt to intrude their own ideas; they interrupt to help the other get back to their original more sincere, yet elusive concerns.

The good listener doesn't moralize. They know their own minds well enough not to be surprised or frightened by strangeness. They know how insane we all are. That's why others can feel comfortable being heard by them. They give the impression they recognize and accept our follies; they don't flinch when we mention a particular desire.

They reassure us they're not going to shred our dignity. A big worry in a competitive world is that we feel we can't afford to be honest about how distressed or obsessed we are. Saying one feels like a failure or a pervert could mean being dropped. The good listener signals early and clearly that they don't see us in these terms. Our vulnerability is something they warm to rather than are appalled by. It is only too easy to end up experiencing ourselves as strangely cursed and exceptionally deviant or uniquely incapable. But the good listener makes their own strategic confessions, so as to set the record straight about the meaning of being a normal (that is very muddled and radically imperfect) human being. They confess not so much to unburden themselves as to help others accept their own nature and see that being a bad parent, a poor lover, a confused worker are not malignant acts of wickedness, but ordinary features of being alive that others have unfairly edited out of their public profiles. When we're in the company of people who listen well, we experience a very powerful pleasure, but too often, we don't really realize what it is about what this person is doing that is so nice. By paying strategic attention to our feelings of satisfaction, we can learn to magnify them and offer them to others, who will notice, heal—and repay the favor in turn. Listening deserves discovery as one of the keys to a good society.

WHISPERING GALLERIES

If you stand alongside the wall inside the dome of St. Paul's Cathedral in London and whisper, someone positioned over 30 meters away can hear you clearly. The circular shape of the wall means that the sound wave of your voice can bounce around and around, delivering secrets to the other side of the dome. Try whispering at an angle to see how far you can make your whisper bounce —think of it like skimming a stone on a lake.

OTHER WHISPERING GALLERIES AROUND THE WORLD:

Grand Central Station, *New York City*

The Rotunda, *San Francisco City Hall, San Francisco*

The Echo Wall, *The Temple Of Heaven, Beijing*

The Bench of Whispers, *Santiago De Compostela, Spain*

Gol Gumbaz, *India*

IN 1969, ELEPHANTS LIVING NEAR
HEATHROW WERE GIVEN EAR MUFFS
TO PROTECT THEM FROM
THE NOISE OF PLANES

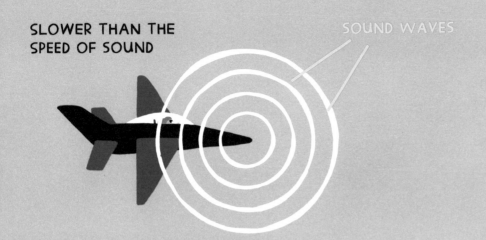

SLOWER THAN THE
SPEED OF SOUND

SOUND WAVES

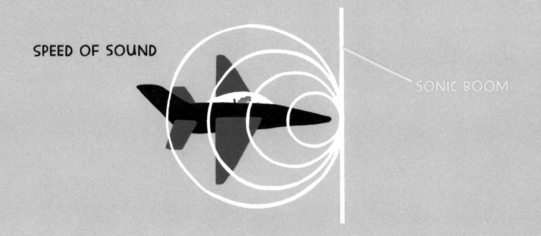

SPEED OF SOUND

SONIC BOOM

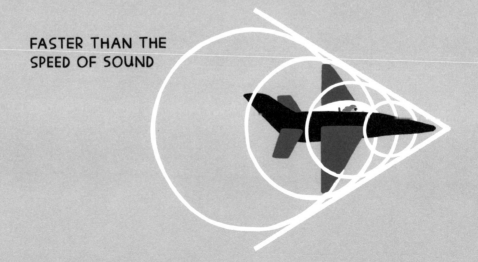

FASTER THAN THE
SPEED OF SOUND

BABABAD

GHTAKAM

NNKONNI

NNERRON

ALGHARA

MINARRO

RONNTO

NTUONN

HUNNTRO
UNAWNS
OHOOHO
THURNUK

OVARRHOU

KAWNTO

ORDENEN

The symbolic thunderclap associated
with the fall of Adam and Eve from Finnegans
Wake by James Joyce.

I get to a small town in Indiana just 15 minutes before the restaurant within the Holiday Inn is closing for the night. I don't feel particularly hungry, even though it is nearly midnight. I am still riding the adrenaline of the 100-mile drive through an unknown darkness alongside semi-trucks.

I'd flipped through the preposterous number of Sirius radio channels before settling on silence. I don't get a lot of silence these days. My darkness is mostly familiar—a baby whimpering in the next room, my husband getting up to go to the bathroom, the homeless folks sorting through the recycling bins outside our bedroom window. It felt good to be hurdling myself through night, alone and on a mission.

My eyes wander over the menu, unsatisfied. *"The chicken wings are really top notch,"* says the man sitting at the bar. A long, rectangular plate filled with chicken wings and onion rings is piled in front of him. He takes a long sip of his beer. He is black, balding, wearing a cranberry velour jumpsuit, looks to be in his 50s.

"Everything is good here," the waitress reassures me. She is young, maybe in her late 20s, wearing a lot of foundation that is even paler than her already pale skin. I'm cynical about her claim, but order the burger and hope for the best. I sit at a tall table, away from the bar, hoping to send the message that I am enjoying my rare solitude.

I end up eavesdropping instead. It's a compulsion.

My previous partner, Nikolai, a born-and-bred New Yorker, tried to teach me how to look into the glass of the subway doors so I could see the reflection of the people I was listening to rather than staring straight at them, but I never got the hang of it. I'm hopeless. I eavesdrop like other people watch reality television, I guess—a little guiltily, but with so much pleasure that I can't resist.

In any case, the chicken wing aficionado clearly isn't a guest of the hotel, but a local who frequents the Holiday Inn for late dinners. He and the waitress have the kind of rapport that evolves over many late nights of shooting the shit. They talk about their love lives. He is gay, struggling to find partners in a town where there isn't a very visible gay community. She is trying to get over a bad man, someone that she knows doesn't deserve her but she loves all the same. They even talk about sex. He's scared to have it again after so long. She'd thought it would make him stay; now she realizes that it's better it didn't.

It's such an intimate conversation. There is so much

shared struggle between these two people who, on paper, would seem to have nothing to talk about—different generations, different races, different genders, different sexual orientations. Yet, here they are, in this small town plunked in the middle of endless cornfields, perched on opposite sides of a hotel bar, just listening to one another talk.

The Center for Courage and Renewal, the organization that Parker Palmer co-founded, has what they call a "touchstone," which basically means a guideline or agreement for a group: *"No fixing, saving, advising, or correcting each other."*

The first time I read it, it sort of took my breath away. So much of our time is spent listening to other people in a doggedly goal-oriented way. Underneath our listening, we're asking ourselves: What can I pluck from what this person is saying that I identify with? What confirms my worldview? What gives me an opportunity to offer advice or a response that will showcase my own intelligence or a chance to share an experience about my life?

I don't mean to make that kind of listening sound shallow or manipulative. Ultimately, it's with great intention that we listen like that. We crave to connect. We crave to be seen. We crave to comfort. It's a very useful kind of listening. It helps us create new nodes, get things done, coalesce within communities.

But there is another kind of listening, a listening that we neglect at our own peril, that is not about getting some particular place, but simply about witnessing another human being. This kind of listening is long and open-ended. It's patient. It's curious. It's not calculating. This kind of listening operates on only one level—the words coming out, the way they hit the ear, the shaping of a story, a sadness, a yearning, a wish.

The guy and the woman in that Holiday Inn, close to midnight on a Monday, were listening like that to one another. Witness over chicken wings. And they made me think about all the people all over the country, sitting in hotel bars and lingering outside of churches and snuggled on living room couches and sitting over steaming cups of tea and maybe even crammed onto airplanes who listen without static or plotting. It's an overlooked kind of love, a way we stay sane. It happens in the cracks, under the radar, just between two people. And it doesn't happen enough.

The burger was surprisingly good. The lesson in listening, totally unexpected.

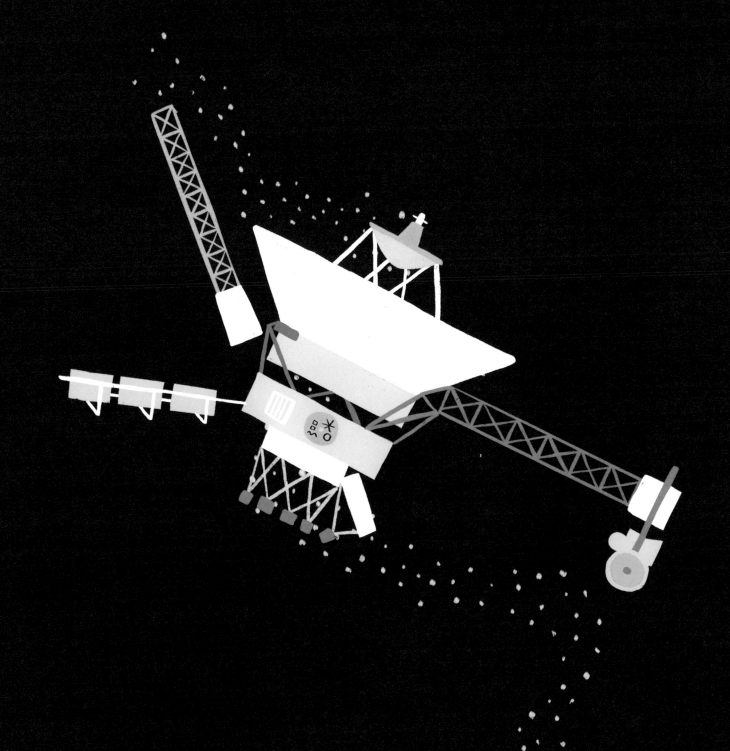

SELECTED CONTENTS OF THE VOYAGER GOLDEN RECORD

Amoy (Min dialect)	"Friends of space, how are you all? Have you eaten yet? Come visit us if you have time."
Arabic	"Greetings to our friends in the stars. We wish that we will meet you someday."
Burmese	"Are you well."
English	"Hello from the children of planet Earth."
Greek	"Greetings to you, whoever you are. We come in friendship to those who are friends."
Gujarati	"Greetings from a human being of the Earth. Please contact."
Indonesian	"Good night ladies and gentlemen. Goodbye and see you next time."
Mandarin Chinese	"Hope everyone's well. We are thinking about you all. Please come here to visit when you have time."
Nyanja	"How are all you people of other planets?"
Oriya	"Greetings to the inhabitants of the universe from the third planet Earth of the star Sun."
Persian	"Hello to the residents of far skies."
Punjabi	"Welcome home. It is a pleasure to receive you."
Rajasthani	"Hello to everyone. We are happy here and you be happy there."
Swedish	"Greetings from a computer programmer in the little university town of Ithaca on the planet Earth"
Ukrainian	"We are sending greetings from our world, wishing you happiness, goodness, good health and many years."

Music of The Spheres

Volcanoes, Earthquake, Thunder

Mud Pots

Wind, Rain, Surf

Crickets, Frogs

Birds, Hyena, Elephant

Chimpanzee

Wild Dog

Footsteps, Heartbeat, Laughter

Fire, Speech

The First Tools

Tame Dog

Herding Sheep,
Blacksmith, Sawing

Tractor, Riveter

Morse Code, Ships

Horse and Cart

Train

Tractor, Bus, Auto

F-111 Flyby,
Saturn 5 Lift-off

Kiss, Mother and Child

Life Signs, Pulsar

Bach, Brandenburg Concerto No. 2 in F. First Movement, Munich Bach Orchestra, Karl Richter, conductor.

Senegal, percussion, recorded by Charles Duvelle

Zaire, Pygmy girls' initiation song

Australia, Aborigine songs, "Morning Star" and "Devil Bird," recorded by Sandra LeBrun Holmes.

"Johnny B. Goode," written and performed by Chuck Berry. 2:38

New Guinea, men's house song, recorded by Robert MacLennan. 1:20

Japan, shakuhachi, "Tsuru No Sugomori" ("Crane's Nest,") performed by Goro Yamaguchi. 4:51

Georgian S.S.R., chorus, "Tchakrulo," collected by Radio Moscow.

Peru, panpipes and drum, collected by Casa de la Cultura, Lima.

"Melancholy Blues," performed by Louis Armstrong and his Hot Seven.

Azerbaijan S.S.R., bagpipes, recorded by Radio Moscow.

"Rite of Spring, Sacrificial Dance," Columbia Symphony Orchestra, Igor Stravinsky, conductor.

"The Well-Tempered Clavier, Book 2, Prelude and Fugue in C, No.1." Glenn Gould, piano, written by Johann Sebastian Bach.

Beethoven, "Fifth Symphony, First Movement," the Philharmonia Orchestra, conducted by Otto Klemperer.

Bulgaria, "Izlel je Delyo Hagdutin," sung by Valya Balkanska.

Navajo indigenous people, "Night Chant," recorded by Willard Rhodes.

Solomon Islands, panpipes, collected by the Solomon Islands Broadcasting Service.

Peru, wedding song, recorded by John Cohen.

China, ch'in, "Flowing Streams," performed by Kuan P'ing-hu.

India, raga, "Jaat Kahan Ho," sung by Surshri Kesar Bai Kerkar.

"Dark Was the Night," written and performed by Blind Willie Johnson.

A golden phonograph record was attached to each of the Voyager spacecraft launched in 1977. One of the purposes of doing so was to send a message to extraterrestrials who might find the spacecraft as it journeyed through interstellar space. In addition to pictures and music and sounds from earth, greetings in 55 languages were included.

NASA asked Dr. Carl Sagan of Cornell University to assemble a greeting and provided him the freedom to choose the format and content to be included. Because of the launch schedule, Sagan (and those he recruited to help him) was not given a lot of time. Linda Salzman Sagan was given the task of assembling the greetings.

The story behind the creation of this "interstellar message" is chronicled in the book, *Murmurs of Earth,* by Carl Sagan, et al. Unfortunately, little information is provided about the individual speakers, many were from Cornell University and surrounding communities. They were given no instructions on what to say other than that it was to be a greeting to possible extraterrestrials and that it must be brief. The following is an excerpt by Linda Salzman Sagan from the book:

"During the entire Voyager project, all decisions were based on the assumption that there were two audiences for whom the message was being prepared—those of us who inhabit Earth and those who exist on the planets of distant stars."

"We were principally concerned with the needs of people on Earth during this section of the recording. We recorded messages from populations all over the globe, each representative speaking in the language of his or her people, instead of sending greetings in one or two languages accompanied by keys for their decipherment. We were aware that the latter alternative might have given the extraterrestrials a better chance of understanding the words precisely, though it would have raised the thorny question of which two languages to send. We felt it was fitting that Voyager greet the universe as a representative of one community, albeit a complex one consisting of many parts. At least the fact that many different languages are represented should be clear from the very existence of a set of short statements separated by pauses and from internal evidence—such as the initial greeting 'Namaste,' which begins many of the greetings from the Indian subcontinent. The greetings are an aural Gestalt, in which each culture is a contributing voice in the choir. After all, by sending a spaceship out of our solar system, we are making an effort to de-provincialize, to rise above our nationalistic interests and join a commonwealth of space-faring societies, if one exists."

"We made a special effort to record those languages spoken by the vast majority of the world's inhabitants. Since all research and technical work on the record had to be accomplished within a period of weeks, we began with a list of the world's most widely spoken languages, which was provided by Dr. Steven Soter of Cornell. Carl suggested that we record the twenty five most widely spoken languages. If we were able to accomplish that, and still had time, we would then try to include as many other languages as we could."

"The organization of recording sessions and the arduous legwork involved in finding, contacting and convincing individual speakers was handled by Shirley Arden, Carl's executive assistant, Wendy Gradison, then Carl's editorial assistant, Dr. Steven Soter, and me. The master table, reproduce on pages 134 through 143, which shows each of the languages, the speaker's name, their comments in the original language, an English translation, and the real and fractional number of human beings who speak that language, was largely Shirley's idea. We contacted various members of the Cornell language departments, who cooperated with us on very short notice and provided numerous speakers, even though school was ending and many people were leaving for summer vacations. Other speakers were more difficult to find. Sometimes it meant sitting for hours, telephoning friends of friends who might know someone who could speak, let's say, the Chinese Wu dialect. After finding such a person, we had to determine whether he or she would be available during the hours when the recording sessions had been scheduled. Even while the recording sessions were going on, we were still trying to find and recruit speakers of languages not yet represented. Often people waiting to record would suggest names of individuals fluent in the very languages we were looking for. Immediately we called those people, explained the project and our plight, and asked them to come at once. Many people did just that."

"Bishun Khare, a senior physicist in the Laboratory for Planetary Studies, was responsible almost single-handedly for the participation of the Indian speakers. He personally called friends and member of the Cornell Indian community, explaining the undertaking to them and asked for and received their cooperation."

"There were only a few disappointments, where someone had agreed to come to a recording session, could not and forgot to let us know in time for us to make other arrangements. It wasn't always possible to find replacements at the last minute, so there are some regrettable omissions —Swahili is one."

"All the greetings, written in the appropriate language, translated to English, and with the name of the speakers, are included in the book. A CD-ROM, which accompanied the 1992 version of the book, included the spoken versions."

YOU CAN USE CRICKETS TO
TELL THE TEMPERATURE.

COUNT THE NUMBER OF CHIRPS IN
25 SECONDS, DIVIDE BY 3, THEN ADD 4.

EG $\frac{48}{3}$ + 4 : 20°C

WHAT DOES UNCONSCIOUS BIAS LOOK LIKE?

Simon Whitaker · January 12, 2017

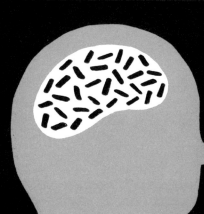

In a recent project meeting we were talking about a technical decision the team had made when implementing a particular feature on iOS. There were four of us in the room: me, an iOS engineer and a PM (all men) and a female TPM. I took a few minutes to explain to the PM and TPM a couple of the fundamentals of iOS development, which helped to explain why we'd taken the direction we had.

After the meeting the TPM asked if she could have a word in private.

"When you explained the technical stuff, was that for my benefit, or the benefit of me and the PM?" she asked.

"It was for both of you," I replied.

"OK, so is there any reason why you only looked at me while you explained it all?"

My gut instinct was to protest; I'm sure I would have looked at both of them in turn as I explained. But I took a moment to think back on the meeting, and she was absolutely right. When I explained the technical stuff, I addressed the explanation to her alone.

About a year ago I took the Managing Unconscious Bias training that Facebook offers. It was fascinating, and it highlighted a number of unconscious biases that I have, including: I have a bias for expecting men to be better at technical subjects and women to be better at arts subjects.

(With a civil engineer for a father and an English teacher for a mother, it doesn't take Freud to figure out where this one came from.)

I remember coming out of that training session feeling as though I'd really learned something useful about myself, but also feeling like I was now automatically a better person because of it. I'd identified and talked openly about my biases! Problem solved!

Yet here I was, a year later, having stumbled straight into the trap my biases had laid.

I thanked the TPM for asking me the question. It took courage to raise the issue, and I wanted first and foremost to acknowledge and validate it. She was right, and it mattered. It mattered not just because I had failed to manage my bias, but because my behavior could actually enforce that same bias in others; a roomful of men just saw me explaining the complicated stuff to the woman in the room.

I also asked her to please continue to keep me on my toes, and to continue highlighting to me any time she saw my biases in action.

Most importantly, I developed a new tactic. I can't conquer my biases, and I shouldn't pretend they don't exist, but I now have a concrete example of how they manifest themselves and I can compensate for that. In meetings, I need to divide my attention and focus equally around the room; especially if I'm explaining technical issues in front of a mixed-gender audience.

Having reflected on this for a few weeks, I'd like to think there are some simple rules that I could follow in future.

Always be open to feedback, especially feedback that pertains to known biases. Not just that; I need to be explicit about the fact that I welcome such feedback, e.g. by writing a note about it. (Told you it would get meta.)

Don't beat myself up about this. These are unconscious biases. I screwed up, but I didn't screw up with malicious intent. Being willing to have the conversation lessens the likelihood of a similar screw up down the road.

Say thank you. It takes courage to give feedback like this, especially feedback that swims upstream against a prevailing power dynamic (e.g. a woman giving feedback to a man; an intern giving feedback to an engineer). The TPM, in finding that courage, has gifted me a valuable, clear, actionable piece of feedback.

Think about strategies to help me counter my biases. For example, in this case I've started making a conscious effort to address everyone in the room equally. It's not easy, but now I have that tactic in my mind I exercise it every opportunity I get.

LISTENING IS THE JOB

Boz · July 7, 2017

"The programmer, like the poet, works only slightly removed from pure thought-stuff. He builds his castles in the air, from air, creating by exertion of the imagination."

— Frederick P Brooks Jr., Mythical Man-Month

While Dr. Brooks was referring specifically to software engineering, I would say his quote applies pretty fairly to all of the work we do at Facebook. Whether marketing, legal, or design, we are all building our castles primarily through exertion of the imagination.

But we aren't limited to our own imagination—we borrow and steal and build upon one another's as well. From interns all the way to Mark Zuckerberg, I don't know anyone at Facebook whose job doesn't hinge upon their ability to acquire information.

If you think it is someone else's job to keep you informed you may be right, but you can take that rightness to the grave for all the good it will do you. The only way to ensure success is to take responsibility for getting the information you need.

Have a System

Don't just consume information opportunistically or at random. Build a rigorous program of what channels you consume, at what frequency, and at what level of depth. For example, I read every email I receive every day. I read every post in a group I'm in every day. If I can't make it through them all, then I know I need to be in fewer groups, on fewer email lists, or involved in less work.

Maximize Signal to Noise Ratio

People are much better at adding channels to consume than they are about removing them, but both are equally important. There is too much information and not enough time to consume it all. Take time to assess your incoming channels, and ask yourself how likely each is to provide you with critical information. Prune channels aggressively when you find you are spending time but rarely getting value. I have a few groups which I scan on a weekly or monthly basis as time permits.

Give Feedback

Do not be a passive consumer. If a channel could be more useful to you then speak up. The person communicating probably wants their effort to be as productive as possible, so they will likely welcome the feedback.

Proactively Identify Gaps

Periodically map out all the people and projects your work depends on. Identify critical channels, and assess if you are getting regular information from those sources. If there aren't any, lobby for them to be established. You'd be surprised how many people are happy to share more information but are unaware there is an interested audience.

Pull the Thread

When you hear something that doesn't match the mental model you have, grab ahold of that thread and see where it leads you. If you let that moment pass, you may be allowing yourself to proceed on the basis of outdated, sub-optimal information. On an average workday I probably write a dozen notes to myself when I hear something that surprises or interests me to make sure I follow up and learn more.

Tell Your Story

This may not sound like a component of listening, but getting your story out is one of the best ways to make sure people inform you when they have relevant information. Good outbound communication is a huge part of getting good inbound communication.

Register Callbacks

When you talk with another team, tell them explicitly the type of information you'd like to receive and establish a contract around it. I consider this step as critical to a successful partnership.

Just Fucking Listen

Stop fighting information and hear what people are telling you. People aren't going to say things as nicely as you want, or with as much data as you want, or with as much understanding as you would like. When you react emotionally or defensively to information, you have a responsibility to introspect on the reasons you are feeling triggered or insecure. Look beyond the rhetoric to find the kernel of valuable feedback to be explored.

By taking responsibility for your information flow, will start to see broader patterns emerge. This won't just make your life easier, it will actually make you better at your job.

TELEPHONES PICTIONARY

A game of interpretation for 5+ players

Required Materials

Small sheets of paper or Post-It notes

Pens or pencils

Gameplay

Players sit around a table. Each player has a stack of paper in front of them.

Players should each numbers the pieces of paper in their stack so they can keep it in order as it is passed around.

Each player writes a phrase on the top page of their stack. This can be as ridiculous or as serious as you want it to be.

Each player passes their stack of paper to the player to their left.

You will receive another player's starting phrase. Move it to the back of the stack, and draw your interpretation of the phrase to the best of your ability.

Pass your stack to the player on your left, with your drawing on top.

You will receive a drawing from the player who gave you the previous phrase. Now, it is your turn to create a phrase interpreting their drawing.

Repeat the drawing-writing stages until you receive your stack. Sometimes, it will be a drawing, sometimes it will be a phrase—it depends on the number of players participating.

Then, take turns sharing your stacks, seeing how well the original phrase stayed intact or how bizarre it has become.

To _____

_____ ?

_____ ?

_____ ?

_____ ?

_____ ?

From _____

_____

_____

_____

_____

_____

_____

_____

To _____

_____ ?

_____ ?

_____ ?

_____ ?

_____ ?

From _____

_____

_____

_____

_____

_____

_____

_____

PLEASE ENJOY THIS MOMENTARY BREAK
THIS PAGE INTENTIONALLY LEFT BLANK

SHUT YOUR EYES AND SEE

Instructions

- Assemble the mask on the previous page
- Set a timer using your phone for three minutes
- Put the mask on and count how many different sounds you can hear
- Write each one down below
- Repeat in two other locations

EXPERIMENT IN PROGRESS

LOCATION 1

_____
_____
_____
_____
_____
_____
_____
_____
_____
_____
_____
_____
_____
_____
_____
_____

LOCATION 2

_____
_____
_____
_____
_____
_____
_____
_____
_____
_____
_____
_____
_____
_____
_____
_____

LOCATION 3

_____
_____
_____
_____
_____
_____
_____
_____
_____
_____
_____
_____
_____
_____
_____
_____

MAKE A RECORD PLAYER

MATERIALS

Sharpened pencil
Pin
Tape
This sheet of paper
Partner
Vinyl record (*one you don't mind experimenting on*)

SCOTCH
TAPE

PIN

ASSEMBLY

Slide the pencil through the center hole of the record so the tip extends an inch or so beyond the other side. Wrap tape around the pencil just below the record, so the pencil stays in place and can't slide back through the center hole. The record should twirl with the pencil.

Cut along the dotted line on this piece of paper. Roll it into a cone shape (using the center marking as a guide) and secure with tape. Push the pin through the tip of the cone around half an inch from the end. It should be at a 45 degree angle.

QUESTIONS TO GET TO KNOW SOMEONE

The best conversations are rivers that ebb and flow with all the twists and turns along the way. It takes practice to hone the skill of conversation so they move along naturally. A collection of good questions in your back pocket can help push you past banal small talk to begin to truly learn about someone—to listen, to hear and understand them in meaningful ways.

Part 1: Starter Questions

What do you do when you're not working?

Did you choose your profession or did it choose you?

What would you do if you won the lottery?

What is your favorite way to relax?

What is your favorite book to read?

What makes you laugh the most?

What is your favorite holiday?

What was the last book you read/movie you saw?

What are your favorite TV shows?

What is one thing you're glad you tried but would never do again?

What do people most often come to you for help for?

Who's your go-to band or artist when you need something to listen to?

What's something you like to do the old-fashioned way?

What is something you have only recently formed an opinion about?

What are you interested in that most people haven't heard of?

What do you think everyone should do at least once in their lives?

What is a cultural obsession you just don't get the point of?

Where is the most interesting place you've been?

What is the luckiest thing that has happened to you?

What is your biggest pet peeve with modern technology?

What object have you been searching for with no luck?

What social customs do you wish would just disappear?

What quirky things do people do where you are from?

Who or where would you haunt if you were a ghost?

Part 2: Deeper Questions

What gets you out of bed every day?

What do you value in a friendship?

What do you say more often in life: yes or no?

What is on your bucket list?

What would you tell your teenage self if you could go back in time?

What mistake do you keep making again and again?

What's the best thing you got from your parents?

What's one responsibility you really wish you didn't have?

What's the best and worst thing about getting older?

What do you regret not doing?

Do you believe in second chances?

Do you want to retire to live or live to retire?

What are some things you wish you could unlearn?

What do you wish your brain was better at doing?

What or who couldn't you live without?

When do you feel the most confident?

What, if anything, about your future would you want to know?

If you could change one decision in your past, what would that be?

What goal are you working on now?

What scares you about the future?

When was the last time you cried?

Do you believe in destiny or in the power of free will?

Who is someone that you miss having in your life?

What question do you always want to ask people but often don't?

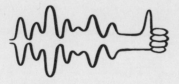

Acknowledgements

A special thank you to the many Facebook employees, friends and others who submitted or provided permission for the reproduction of their work as part of this project.

This book was produced as part of the Designer in Residence program in the Facebook Analog Research Lab in Menlo Park, California.

FACEBOOK ANALOG RESEARCH LAB

1 Hacker Way Menlo Park, CA 94025

f facebook.com/analoglab   instagram.com/analoglab

ISBN: 978-0-9965642-3-6
ISBN: 0-9965642-3-3

Best enjoyed outdoors surrounded by the sounds of nature, on a train, a rooftop, or at home in your favorite chair.

Designed by Fuchsia MacAree and Scott Boms
Illustrations by Fuchsia MacAree
Copyediting & Proofreading by Kristin Farr

Printed and bound in Canada by Hemlock Printers Ltd.

Colophon

Metric by Kris Sowersby, *klim.co.nz*
Scotch by Neil Summerour, *positype.com*
Listening by Fuchsia MacAree, *macaree.ie*

First Edition, 2017

Citations

"Communication is the Job" and *"Listening is the Job"*
  by Andrew "Boz" Bosworth

"Information Diversity & Unfollowing"
  by Lada Adamic

"I am Listening"
  by Ramya Sethuraman

"Interrupting"
  by Debbie Ferguson

*"Removing People who Have Died
  from Insensitive Product Experiences"*
  by Moira Burke

"How to be a good listener" from The Book of Life
  Copyright © 2016 The School of Life/Alain de Botton
  Source: *thebookoflife.org/how-to-be-a-good-listener*

"Listening in the Cracks" from On Being
  Copyright © 2015 On Being/Courtney E. Martin
  Source: *onbeing.org/blog/listening-in-the-cracks*

"Transitscapes" photography by Christian Palino
  Source: *instagr.am/christianpalino*

"What Does Unconscious Bias Look Like?"
  by Simon Whitaker